INSIGHTS

for the

SPORTS COACH

PAUL KILGANNON

Book Interior, Book Cover and E-book formatting by Amit Dey (amitdey2528@gmail.com)
Illustrator: Lucia Balazova

ISBN: 978-1-7384661-3-9 (Hardcover)
ISBN: 978-1-7384661-4-6 (Softcover)
ISBN: 978-1-7384661-5-3 (E-book)

For further information re international distribution, or to contact Paul Kilgannon regarding speaking engagement or consultation contact: info@carvercoachingframework.com

www.carvercoachingframework.com
X & Instagram: @carver_coaching
Facebook: Carver Coaching
Youtube: @CarverCoaching
LinkedIn: @PaulKilgannon

Contents

About Paul Kilgannon

Hi, I'm Paul. I'm married to Lauren, have a baby son called Rían and a dog called Ruby. I live in Galway, on the west coast of Ireland. It is beautiful here; you should come visit. I work as a *Performance Coach*, I write stuff and I created *The CARVER Coaching Framework* which is used internationally across a number of sports, educational settings and workplaces.

Through my company *CARVER Coaching and Performance*, I provide a consultancy service, and a variety of coaching supports to: coaches and leaders, athletes and performers, teams, clubs and organisations across numerous sports and beyond.

I like to say that *'performance is omnipresent and coaching is ever optional'* and so the principled nature of my work allows me to help across many domains.

I believe strongly in a positive, holistic approach to coaching in sport, and that lessons learned in sport can, and must, positively contribute to all areas of life. I *know* Coach Development to be the single most important agent for change in sport, and all performance domains.

Viva La Revolution,
Paul

What is The *CARVER Framework?*

The CARVER Framework is a conceptual coaching framework that enables the coach to *'build their coaching world'* and practice continuous improvement in their coaching.

CARVER is an acronym containing the elements of: *Connection, Awareness, Research, Values and Visions, Endorsing and Reflection.*

Coaching is often referred to as a craft, and like all crafts it consists of three elements: *perspective, skills and tools.* Michelangelo was one of the most skilled craftsmen of all. He was a carver and famously said of his masterpiece David:

> *"I saw the angel in the marble and carved until I set him free."*

The CARVER Framework harnesses *these concepts and* positions coaching as a craft where the challenge is simply to get the best out of people. *It* offers the coach a set of highly usable *lenses, tools and skills.*

The CARVER Framework is domain agnostic, in that its principles and teachings are applicable to all performance environments. *The Framework* strives to encapsulate and explain coaching in a simple, intuitive and engaging manner.

What is a *CARVER Insight?*

A *CARVER Insight* is an essay crafted with the purpose of challenging and inspiring you, the sports coach. A *CARVER Insight* strives to impact your thinking and positively influence your coaching practice.

As time allows, find a little space in your life, engage with an *Insight*, and make your own of it. Each essay should serve as a lens through which you can examine and refine your coaching philosophy and practice, and ultimately, your impact on those you coach and lead.

There is no particular order to follow in reading these *Insights*. I suggest you take a look at the essay titles in the *Contents* and see what speaks to you at that moment in time.

.⧽⧼.

I want you to keep this book close by you. It is a *'pick up and put down'* type of book. It should be thought provoking. There are blank pages for you to write, reflect and get out onto paper what is in your head.

Use the *CARVER Insights* to develop your intuition. Intuition is key to authentic coaching. Too many coaches fall into the trap of trying to be someone else. To quote the American Philosopher and Author Joseph Campbell.

*"The privilege of a lifetime is being
who you are."*

These *Insights* are designed to navigate you towards your *'Best Self'* in coaching. Your athletes will love you at *your* best.

Every coach is at a different stage of their own coaching evolution. No path is the same, so read and reread these essays over time. The Ancient Greek Philosopher Heraclitus said:

> *"No man ever steps in the same river twice, for it's not the same river and he's not the same man."*

And so, although the words on these pages will not change, I am confident that as you read and reread them, what they are saying to you, will.

Who is the book for?

This book is for anyone who sees themselves as a coach. It is primarily written for sports coaches, but much of the content is applicable to coaches across all performance domains.

For Rían, and in memory of
Owen Kilgannon (RIP).

Rían and Owen December 2023

"Choose not a life of imitation…"
Can't Stop (Red Hot Chili Peppers)

What do you Know for Sure ...?

I help coaches and leaders across multiple sports and many working environments. One exercise I like to complete, and continually revisit with coaches is the… *'What do you know for sure about coaching?'.* It's a simple exercise, but then again…simplicity yields complexity. I know that for sure!

Coaching is not rocket science. To the contrary, it is in fact pretty intuitive. It is a relatively simple practice. If we take the time to contemplate and self-search, we will find that most of the answers lie within.

I adopted the *'what do you know for sure about coaching'* exercise from the *'Queen of the Talk Show',* Oprah Winfrey. I guess part of the reason she was so good at her job was because she asked questions which got to the core of people. *"What do you know for sure?"* was a question she posed to countless of her interviewees. She also wrote a weekly column, and later a book titled *"What I Know for Sure".*

In asking this question, Oprah was seeking to find the interviewees *'personal truths.'* A *'personal truth'* is a belief or perspective that an individual holds as true, based on their own experiences and interpretations. *'Personal truths'* are subjective, and can be heavily influenced by a person's culture, values and beliefs. These *truths* may not be verifiable or universally accepted. However, they shape an individual's understanding of the world and their place in it, and can act

Most of the answers lie within.

as a decision-making framework for them. They can act as a prism through which they view the world.

.∽🙠∾.

I like coaches to use this concept, and I like them to actively evolve and refine their *'personal truths'* as they grow in their coaching. It is an iterative process.

Coaching entails, the ceaseless pursuit of figuring out what is no longer important. Life is complex. There are many decisions to be made. Circumstances push and pull the coach in different directions. Developing *'personal truths'*, mantras or a credo can be powerful stuff.

For me, building a coaching philosophy around *'personal truths'* or *'what you know for sure about coaching'* is a great basis for security. If the coach spends high-quality time developing and refining appropriate *'truths'*, and then goes on to honour and live them, we can be pretty much guaranteed that our work will be impactful. To the contrary, when our work goes awry, more often than not, it is as direct result of deviating from a fundamental truth, i.e. *something we know for sure*.

As mere mortals we are designed to drift. Human nature is always working against us. I find Oprah's favourite question to be a mighty *anchor* or *North Star* for coaches. These *'truths'* can also act as a decision-making framework for us to utilise when faced with challenge.

I have been gathering my list of *'what I know for sure about coaching'* for many years now. Originally, I used to share my Top 20 at the beginning of my key-note talks, and explain each one in detail. Now, I share 10 of them at the end, and the hope is that I will have mentioned all of them in some form or other throughout the talk, thus modelling the value of the exercise.

In no particular order, here are 3 of my *'truths'*.

What I Know for Sure About Coaching:

- *When coaching athletes, I don't have to like them all, but I have to love them all.* (I took this one from the great John Wooden).
- *Environment is the silent hand of behaviour.*
- *The most important thing, is to keep the most important thing, the most important thing.*

What are your *'truths'*? What do you know for sure about coaching?

Go figure!

Determining and Detailing
Your Visions

The American agricultural scientist and inventor, George Washington Carver, once said:

"Where there is no vision, there is no hope."

Born a slave, Carver went on to be one of the most prominent black scientists of the early 20th century. He taught as the first black faculty member at Iowa State, and went on to become head of the Agriculture Department at what is now Tuskegee University, where he taught for 47 years.

Carver was a visionary. He designed a mobile classroom in order to take education out to the farmers in the fields. He shared with these poor farmers, techniques he had developed to improve soils depleted by their repeated planting of cotton. He urged these farmers to restore nitrogen to their soils by practicing systematic crop rotation; alternating cotton crops with plantings of sweet potatoes or legumes, such as peanuts, soybeans and cowpeas. These crops both restored nitrogen to the soil and were good for human consumption. Following his crop rotation, practice resulted in improved cotton yields, and provided the farmers with alternative cash crops. In order to train the farmers to successfully rotate and cultivate their new crops, Carver developed an agricultural extension programme for

Where there is no vision, there is no hope.

Alabama. Following this, he widely distributed recipes using these alternative crops, thereby encouraging better nutrition in the South.

His work became famous all over the world, and his influence was profound. He became affectionately known as the Peanut Man having discovered over 300 uses for the peanut including use in: shaving cream, shampoo, wood stains, and plastics. He also came up with an incredible number of edible options for the product. Through his ground-breaking achievements in agriculture, Carver both improved the economic conditions of African Americans in the South, and paved the way for greater African-American representation in science. His vision was to enrich his people's lives. He worked to transform science into products that would benefit the lives of black rural people.

Like all good teachers and coaches, Carver was as much concerned with his students' character development, as he was with their intellectual development. To clarify his thinking, he compiled a list of *"eight cardinal virtues"* whose possession defines *"a lady or a gentleman"*:

- *Be clean, both inside and out.*
- *Who neither looks up to the rich, nor down on the poor.*
- *Who loses, if needs be, without squealing.*
- *Who wins, without bragging.*

- *Who is always considerate of women, children and old people.*

- *Who is too brave to lie.*

- *Who is too generous to cheat.*

- *Who takes his share of the world, and lets other people have theirs.*

George Washington Carver died on January 5th 1945. The epitaph on his tombstone reads:

"He could have added fortune to fame, but caring for neither, he found happiness and honor in being helpful to the world."

.·~ৎᎦৎᎦ~·.

'Visions' is one of the 'V's' of *The CARVER Framework*; with *Values* being the other one. *The Framework* positions 'Values and Visions' as the core of one's Coaching Philosophy.

Like George Washington Carver, the prudent coach has many *Visions* which may include:

- A *Vision* for the type of coach they want to be.

- A Vision for the Sporting and Non- Sporting Qualities of their Players.

- A Vison for their Team.

- A Vision for Success and Winning.

- A Vision for their Coaching Team.
- A Vision for the 'emotive state' in which they want their players to play in.
- A Vision for their style of play or Game Model.

To quote Caver,

"Where there is no vision, there is no hope."

What are your *Visions*?

Go figure!

Changing Perspective

I received a lovely message from a man called Jim last week. I had recently given a talk to his club and his message inferred that my presentation had changed many of the attendees' perspective on coaching. That is my job... to help people change the way they look at things. My job is to educate people's perspective.

The CARVER Framework was designed as a set of lenses through which to view coaching; a perspective, so to speak. On page 10 of my first book *'Coaching Children in Sport- The CARVER Framework'* I wrote,

> *'Perspective is hugely important. If you change the way you look at things, the things you look at change.'*

So when Jim used the word *"perspective"*, it resonated.

Now for a bit of a story...

When I wrote that first book, I was an extremely green and inexperienced writer. I worked so hard on it, that I still get a physical pain in my head when I think back to that time. Building *The CARVER Framework* and ensuring it included all that was necessary, and nothing else, was painstaking work. I literally had to write a coaching book into a conceptual acronym which

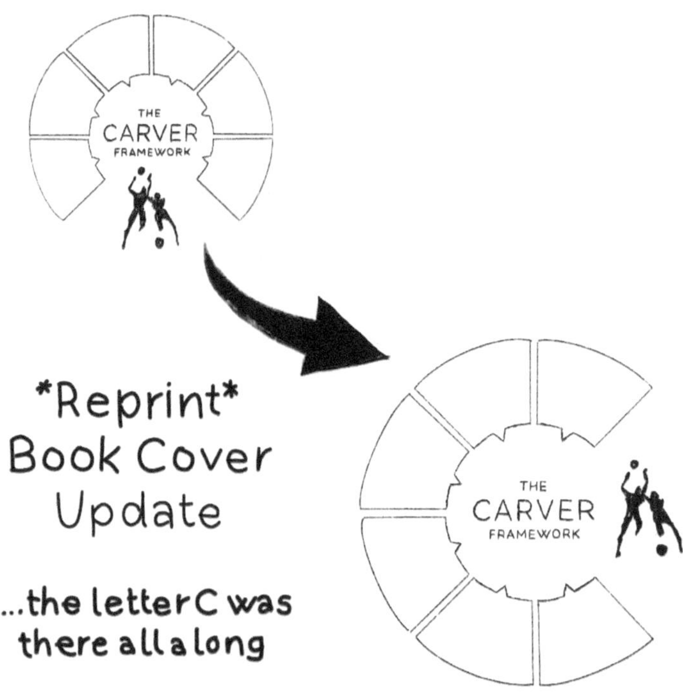

Reprint
Book Cover
Update

...the letter C was
there all along

If you change the way you look at things, the things you look at change.

predetermined, or constrained, the chronological order of the content. Anyone who has read that book, or seen and heard me present on the CARVER Framework, may well appreciate the complexity of this challenge.

That book took me about three years to write, but like most things, it was rushed towards the end. When the book was released, I was disappointed that there was a number of typos in it. Fortunately, the first run sold out more or less straight away, so there was a scramble to reprint it. This offered me a short window to sort the typos. I gave the book to Fran, a trusted head, and told him I needed it forensically proofed, and all the typos highlighted. Fran was the man for the job, and got to it promptly. I met him a few days later when he had finished, and as he handed me back the book he jokingly said that my biggest error was on the front cover.

As he handed the original book back to me, he turned it sideways and said, *"If you turn it sideways, you'll have a 'C'."*

I had spent 3 years writing the book; The name of which was the CARVER Framework. Its subject matter was *Coaching Children*. It was book orientated around concepts such as: *Craft, Competence, Confidence, Contribution, Caring, Connection, Creativity, Challenge* and so on. It was a book about changing people's perspective, and yet I couldn't see that if I rotated the icon on the front cover 90 degrees it would make the letter *'C'*. It was literally under my nose, but my perspective was off, and I couldn't see it.

.ᴄᴏᴏ.

Perspective is key in both coaching and life. Sometimes you can look at things for so long and fail to see what is staring you in the face. Then once you see it… it cannot be unseen.

'Perspective is key…Can you see?'
(I actually wrote that on Page 11 of that book)

Where in your coaching practice might you benefit from a change of perspective?

Go figure!

Making the Desired Behaviours More Attractive

My friend is a Quare Hawk *(a term of affection used in the west of Ireland for someone who is unique).* In fact, he is such a Quare Hawk, that his nickname is, *'The Quare Hawk'*...or *'The Hawk'* for short. Some years back, in an audacious bid to manoeuvre his way into a nightclub in Dublin, he fell and hurt his back while climbing *("scaling")* a wall. We called the whole episode, *"Quare Hawk Down".* He truly is a character!

'The Hawk' claims to have *"no interest"* in sport and even less interest in coaching. He *'doesn't believe'* in books, podcasts, blogs or newsletters. He is a great guy, and one of my oldest and dearest friends.

Last week, he asked me to give him a hand with a couple of horses he has. I love helping with physical tasks as there is great sense of freedom in it for me.

As myself and *'The Hawk'* went out to his yard, I noticed his horsebox was backed into the entrance to his stables. Either side of the horsebox, he had placed a free standing gate to close off the gap. In truth, it was a rough enough set up!

Anyway...both the back ramp and side door of the horsebox were left open. As a result of this elaborate set-up, the horses had to walk up one ramp and down another one if they wished to go out to the field from the stable or, indeed, vice versa. This was a journey they would make at least twice a day.

Yes, *'The Hawk'* was training the horses to load into the horsebox, and unknown to himself he was utilising the *Constraints Led Approach*. As I commended him on the sophistication of his pedagogical approach, he went on to impress me further with the rationale behind his technique.

In non-academic language, he explained very clearly how he was *'constraining to afford'*. He wasn't telling or forcing, rather he was making the desired behaviours more obvious or attractive to the horses. He had created an environment that challenged the horses to figure things out on their own. He had promoted *exploration* and *self-organistion*. Specific skills or behaviours were developing organically. His role was simply to engineer an environment that would facilitate learning through *exploration, adaptation,* and *self-organisation*, ultimately leading to more skilled and adaptable horses. Intuitively, he understood and appreciated learning to be an *emergent behaviour.* Genius stuff from *'The Hawk'* indeed…and boy was he proud of himself!

I won't go into the *Constraints Led Approach* to coaching in detail here, but what I will do is to challenge you to think like *'The Hawk'.* Ask yourself: *How can I engineer or manipulate the environment in order to make the desired behaviours more attractive to my athletes?'*

If *'The Hawk'* can do it, then you can too.

Go figure!

The Hawk's Set-Up.

Focusing on What is of Primary Importance

Occasionally I have ideas or concepts in my head, and am unsure whether I have come up with them myself, or if I have seen them elsewhere. When sharing the analogy of the *'Primary Colours of Performance'* with a buddy some time back, he asked if I had come up with it myself, and I replied that I thought I had. He said I should trademark it...or something of the like. Obviously this would take some doing, and in any case I'm not really sure if the concept is mine in the first place. Anyways...here goes...and if it does end up to be my idea and it takes off, well at least I will have it here in print. (If not, please inform me of the source ☺).

'Colour Theory' teaches us that primary colours of red, yellow and blue are the building blocks for all other colours. They are the basic colours that cannot be created by mixing other colours. When you mix two primary colours, you get secondary colours:

- Red + Yellow = Orange
- Yellow + Blue = Green
- Blue + Red = Purple

When you mix a primary colour with a neighbouring secondary colour, you get tertiary colours. Examples include:

- Red + Orange = Red-Orange
- Yellow + Green = Yellow-Green
- Blue + Purple = Blue-Purple

Black is used to create a shade, while white is used to create tints. Pure grey, consisting of a combination of black and white, is added to a colour (hue) to create a tone.

In brief, all colours emerge from the primary colours. Variables of a colour, come into play through black and white.

.⤳᠔ℓᔆᤢ.

So where am I going with all this…

A critical element of coaching involves driving competitive performance in our athletes and teams. In preparing our charges to perform we are frequently challenged to come up with engaging ways to help them appreciate, and focus on, what truly drives competitive performance.

Sporting performance can be defined as the delivery of trained capabilities. Such capabilities are already there in advance of competition, but are waiting to emerge in the correct conditions, and with the appropriate focus of attention. It should be self-evident that these capabilities will be determined by the level of preparation, but that said, the collective focus of the group is critical.

In the lead up to competition the analogy of the *'Primary Colours of Performance'* can be used to focus a team's attention on what is of primary importance. In other words: What are the three *'primary drivers'* for delivering performance? The trick is to imagine each of the primary colours (red, yellow and blue) as representing the key skills or qualities the team need to focus on. All other *'colours'* (skills and qualities) can only emerge in the presence of the *'primary colours'*.

In a workshop type activity in advance of competition, players can be facilitated to discuss and debate what are the *'red, yellow, and blue'* they need to deliver in order to create all other *'colours'* (these will vary from game to game).

By applying this analogy, coaches can help guide their teams to concentrate on three fundamental elements, trusting that all other aspects of performance will emerge from the interaction of these core qualities or components. In other words, focusing on three foundational elements can lead to the emergence of a complete and balanced performance. These *'primary colours'* become the team's collective focus before, and indeed, during competition. *'White and black'* are, of course, the colours of management i.e. tactical formations, personnel selection, etc.

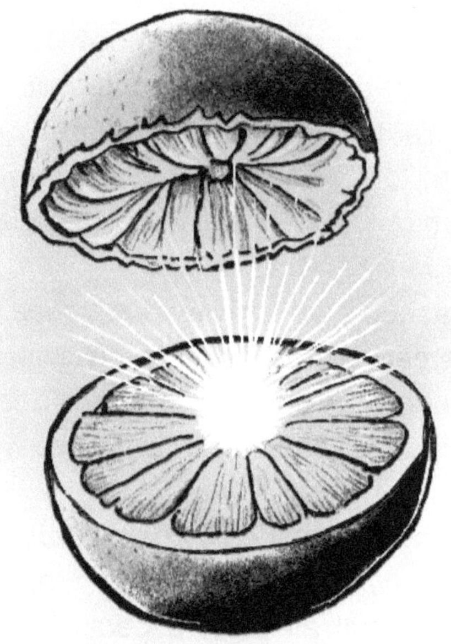

Coaching and performance entail getting to the essence of things.

.ᴄ∾ᵥᴏᵥᴇᴐ.

Coaching and performance entail getting to the essence of things. Often as coaches and athletes we put our attention on things that are *secondary* at best. Indeed, the irony is that these things will emerge if we place our focus on what is of primary importance.

The key is to place the focus on *'red, yellow and blue'* and trust that *the 'greens, blues, purples and so on'* will take care of themselves. As coaches, we must be ready to add the *'black and white'* as required. Soon you may well see the whole *colour pallet* emerge.

The *'red, yellow and blue'* analogy can be used and adapted in all coaching, performance, and indeed life, scenarios. High performance across all domains requires effectively executing what is of *'primary importance'*.

How might you use this analogy in your coaching practice?

Go figure!

Winning the Relationship Game

A couple of weeks back, I caught up with a coaching buddy whose team have recently reached the pinnacle of their sport. Over the past few seasons, they have been successful at local level, winning six consecutive county titles. However, they have consistently come up short on the national stage. My question to him was simple: *What had they done differently this year?*

His answer was that they had put a huge emphasis on one-to-one meetings and conversations; they had put a strong emphasis on building relationships with the individual. He said that he felt that putting this time into the individual, had helped build the trust required for them to take on huge challenges together.

Coaching is a relationship between two people. Even in a large group setting, coaching is still a relationship between two people. Each individual requires attention in a different way and the challenge for the diligent coach and management team is to understand how and when to deliver the individualised support needed. To achieve this, the coach must get to know each individual. When we appreciate this, we come to understand that the relationship game may well be the first game we must win as coach.

.⤳⤳.

Catering for the needs of the individual in the team environment is challenging, but critical. An unquestionable truth is that teams only thrive when people do. To quote Oprah Winfrey,

> *"We all want to be valued. We all want*
> *to be seen. We all want to know*
> *that we matter."*

The essence of coaching is making those you coach feel valued and important. This connection will precede true engagement, commitment and contribution. As per the fifth of Stephen Covey's The 7 Habits of Highly Effective People we must *'seek first to understand, then be understood'*.

Our challenge is to create meaningful and impactful conversations. The prudent coach is always asking, "How do I create more meaningful conversations?" We must have an aspiration to be great at relationships. Communication and trust are key to relationships, but we cannot have trust without communication.

Coaching is all about the individual; the person. Build the person, and with the correct input the performer will flourish. Great coaches have an ability to build belief in those they coach, to empower them to attain their full potential. They help develop the athlete's want towards self-improvement; their disposition towards themselves.

> *"Phil was more than just a coach to me.*
> *He was a mentor and a father figure.*
> *He taught me how to play within the team,*

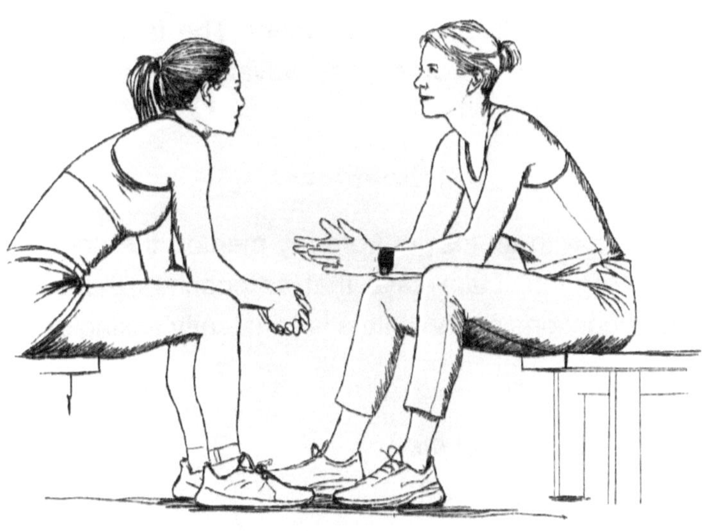

The relationship game may well be the first game you must win as coach.

> *how to lead, and how to think about*
> *the game in ways I never had before.*
> *His guidance was critical in my development*
> *as both a player and a person."*

Kobe Bryant on Phil Jackson

The key is to *'get to'* the individual and this is challenging in a collective environment. The fact that it is hard, makes it a competitive advantage by its very nature.

.⦿.

I will end with an insight from my mentor, the great Dr Liam Moggan. Liam says that as coaches there are three questions every athlete is constantly asking of us:

1. *Do you like me?*
2. *Can you help me?*
3. *Can I trust you?*

I often use this with coaches, but have adapted Question 1 to be: *Do you love me?* Because to quote John Wooden,

> *"You don't have to like them all, but you*
> *have to love them all."*

During the one-to-one conversations my buddy had with his players throughout the year, he was answering all these questions for them.

What questions do you feel you need to answer for your athletes?

Go figure!

Appreciating One's Influence

I keep a medal in my wallet that simply states: *'Your influence in never neutral'*. I was given it at *The Way of Champions* coaching conference a number of years back. I'd lie if I said I notice it every day, but I keep it there as an anchor of sorts. When dealing with people, a leader's influence is never neutral. We are either making the situation better, or worse, to varying degrees.

I worked as a primary school teacher for fifteen years. I enjoyed my time teaching; together with the children, we had great days. Much of what I know about coaching, I learned from teaching. In truth, coaching and teaching are one and the same. Or, at least, on the same continuum.

Fifteen years of teaching is a lot of children, and a lot of opportunities to influence in a positive manner provided one has the appropriate skills and levels of self-awareness. About 3 years ago, I received a call from the father of a girl I had taught in third class, many years previously. He has just left his daughter to college for her first day as a medical student and rang to share with me that on the way to the college he had asked his daughter why she had chosen medicine as a career path. She replied that it was something I had said to her, while she was with me in third class, that had lit the flame. Recently while in town with my wife, we met that father and his daughter. It was great

Your influence in never neutral.

to meet them, and she is now thriving as a third year medical student.

I write this piece to both personally reflect on, and share with you, the power of influence. Eckhart Tolle's quote, *"Awareness is the greatest agent for change"* always resonates with me. All too often we simply don't know, what we don't know, and therefore we can't change our behaviour. I want both you and I, to be (more) aware of our influence as coaches.

Our challenge, and indeed our responsibility, is to help people see the best in themselves; to help them see the possibility this world has to offer them. No one is perfect, and highlighting imperfections…well let's just say, I'm sure there is enough people out there doing that.

Build on people's strengths as opposed to highlight their weaknesses. Notice the positive. A kind and considered word of encouragement can go a long way and can have many unintended positive consequences. To paraphrase the American Historian Henry Adams,

> *'A coach affects eternity; they can never tell where their influence stops.'*

Your influence is never neutral.

What influence do you wish to have on your people?

Go figure!

Creating a Giving Environment

My wife has a great faith in God and is a strong and active Christian. When she moved here from Texas to live with me, we began to attend *The Church of Discovery Galway* on a consistent basis. In coaching and performance parlance, let's just say…I am not as talented a Christian as my wife and although not new to the game, it is fair to say I have missed a lot of training and have work to do. Having gone to church week on week for a consistent period, I have observed first-hand and marvelled at how an exceptional environment has been crafted and sustained.

Firstly, we are greeted at the main door by two smiling faces, and two further smiling faces just inside. Name badges are often used, and church often begins with a shake of hands and *'hello'* to those around you. Each day, a circa 8-piece band plays 2 songs to begin. There are drums, guitars, keyboards and so on. The music is powerful and uplifting. Everyone sings along as the words are projected onto a big screen. Different groups perform each week; all god's children have a place in the choir. There is opportunity for anyone with interest.

The Pastor's name is Paul. He is warm, relatable, knowledgeable and humble. It is obvious he cares deeply about his Church and its people. He frequently talks about the purpose of the church, and what he wants it to embody. His sermons are considered, relatable and from the heart. Guest pastors often preach; both male and female, black and white, young and old. There is example and role models for all, as Pastor Paul frequently steps aside in order to allow new people opportunity for growth. He is a leader who facilitates growth.

A team of people help with the lighting, videography and technology, while another team provide food and refreshments for those who stay to catch up afterwards. A prayer team is on hand for anyone who needs prayer. Counselling is provided for those in need of help. People bring their unique skills and talents and make things better; everyone can help, there is a job for everyone and the needs of the people are met. The children attend the *'Children's Church'* which is upstairs, and volunteers lead this in an age-appropriate manner. The teenagers also have their own time together on a Friday evening.

Throughout the week there are various activities and gatherings: music lessons, training, bible studies and so on. People's competencies are grown, and so they are enabled to contribute at a higher level. The conveyer belt is constantly churning out skilled people who are competent, confident and motivated to contribute to the environment. Once a month, the ladies meet for dinner in the church on a Friday, and have themed evenings. The last one was 'African' evening…my wife had a great time. The men also meet in the church once a month, on a Saturday, and share breakfast together.

People gather in family homes during the week as part of *'connect groups'*. They share their troubles and

An effective leader facilitates growth.

hardships, and support each other. The diversity in the groups is amazing. This humbles people who have the capacity to be humbled, and gives one a great insight into how other people live. We are all the same really.

.⁓৹৹⁓.

So what you ask has all this got to do with coaching and performance? Week on week I have observed a vibrant atmosphere and environment where people come with a sense of purpose, willing and able to contribute to the greater good. They come to serve and be served; they come to help. It is through giving that they receive. The environment is engineered in a way that drives such behaviour. Everyone can contribute in their own way. They have choice, opportunity, competency and they feel related to the purpose and mission… *The Self Determination Theory* in practice. The environment drives the most desirable behaviour of all: Contribution!

So, as I observe with my coaching hat on, I continue to ask myself how can I create an environment within my team where people both want, and are enabled, to give the best of themselves.

I have said it before and I may well say it again… coaching and performance are principle based practices.

What lessons can you take from this exceptional learning and development environment?

Go figure!

Shepherding the Flock

Some years back, I was involved in helping to coach a team that were very close to achieving, what for them would have been, their *'Holy Grail'*. They were a small club who, to many were overachieving. In some ways they were the *'peoples' champions'*. They had lost out in the final stages of their competition for a number of years in a row. They really felt like it was within touching distance. The team were ambitious and *'wanted it'*.

Their style of play was fast, intense and instinctive. From my perspective, they were a team that were willing to work hard, but there was something of an unconscious resistance to taking a breath, and looking at the granularity of *'working smart'*. Working smart can often be tedious and slow moving in the short term. It can often feel cumbersome, and counter intuitive. My feeling was that in order for this team to move forwards, they might first have to at least pause, or perhaps take a step backwards. They couldn't simply keep doing what they were doing and be confident it would improve their plight. I felt a slight change of approach was necessary. I believed they couldn't simply keep *'pushing'*.

My challenge was to articulate my thoughts in a way that would resonate with the players. They needed to believe in the proposed change. In a fit of inspiration, or perhaps desperation, I began to write a fable. The team was full of tradesmen and manual workers, so I began to write a fable about a small building contractor who had started to win great contracts in the *'big city'* and all of his peers thought he had *'made it'*. However, the reality was that he wasn't making any money, because he hadn't the correct processes in place, and hadn't the required attention to detail in his work flow. It was one thing to be getting, and doing great work, and of course that would receive plaudits and recognition, but he was in the business of making money.

Long story short, I never finished writing that fable and so I never delivered it to the team. The team failed to make significant progress that year. Sport is tough; as is coaching.

I read back over that effort at a fable this week, as I began my second attempt to write one.

Here goes...

.᷒ೢ᷎.

This is *'The Fable of the Two Shepherds'*

Two shepherds, Joe and Jim, were each given a flock of 30 sheep by a village, to rare on a nearby mountain. The village's people were good people, who loved animals and had a great appreciation of shep-herding. The sheep were young and vulnerable.

'Shepherd Joe' loved all of his sheep, and minded every one of them as best he could. He slowed down for the slow ones, and sorted extra grass for the weak ones. He also looked after the strong ones, and met their needs as best he could. Occasionally, he

Love them all!

separated some that were butting heads. It wasn't an exact science. Often it was trial and error.

Joe worked from a simple philosophy which was, 'love them all'. If one was sick, he cared for them and if one was lost, he went looking for them. He operated from a place of love, and created a loving environment that met the needs of all his sheep, as best as possible. In brief, all the sheep were loved.

Joe was a humble and open-minded shepherd, who learned as he went. If he met another shepherd on the mountain, he would ask them some questions and listen intently to their answers. To begin, Joe wasn't the most skilled or knowledgeable shepherd but he was open to learning and so improved as he went. Joe's big strength was that he was coming from the right place. His mantra of *'love them all'* shaped how he approached his work.

.⁓꘎⁓.

'Shepherd Jim' had a different philosophy, although he hadn't taken the time to contemplate and reflect on it, or indeed articulate it. In essence, his philosophy was *'love the lovely ones'*. Jim hadn't much time for the slow, or the weak sheep. His interest lay in the strong ones, the ones that caught the eye. Although an experienced shepherd, Jim was somewhat arrogant, and thought he knew it all. He had little regard for his fellow shepherds. He felt he knew more than them, and could learn little from them.

.ᴄᘔᕟᘔᴄ.

After a few of years on the mountain, both shepherds were summoned to return to the village with their flock. *'Shepherd Joe'* returned with all 30 of his sheep. It was an impressive flock. All of the sheep had grown and developed. Sure, some were bigger than others, but all had more of less reached their physical potential. Surprisingly to Joe, and indeed the villagers, some of the flock that were originally small and weak, had turned into the *'biggest and best'*, while some of the original *'biggest and best'* had stagnated as they aged. Joe came to learn that they had simply been early maturers.

'Shepherd Jim' returned with less than half of his flock. Sure, some of them were big and beautiful, but many of the others were quite ordinary. Indeed, Jim had ended up being disappointed in some of the sheep that had originally been bigger and stronger than the rest. He had put so much time into them and they hadn't developed as he had expected.

When Jim saw Joe with his full and impressive flock he began to lament some of the sheep he had lost along the way in the mountain. He thought back to a number of occasions, where he had been so focused on the *'good ones'* that the *'weak ones'* had simply strayed off, and disappeared. He wondered if some of these *'weak ones'* who had strayed would have fared better long term, and surpassed the original *'good ones'*.

On their return to the village, it was announced that there was to be a vote among the village people as to who the *'Best Shepherd'* was. It was a landslide victory.

Which Shepherd do you think won?

Go figure!

Using Song to Excite and Unite

I took my first adult coaching role at 26 years old. I was young, and it was with my own senior hurling team; among my peers and indeed elders (we were an ageing team). It was a deeply personal mission. I loved my club, and many of the older players had been heroes of mine growing up. Our team had been regressing for a number of years. The relegation playoff had become our perennial home. In my first year as coach it took me some time to get my concepts across to the players, but by the end of that year we were finding form. We still found ourselves in a relegation battle, but we came through it in some style, and it was clear to all we were making progress.

In the pre-season of Year 2, we travelled by bus to climb Croagh Patrick in County Mayo on the west coast of Ireland. This was one of a number of activities we did in a bid to build unity in the group. On the way back up the road in the bus, we got our hands on the microphone, and a number of the lads sang. There was no alcohol involved; just good clean fun.

We won our first round championship game that year, and this was our first time in over 5 years to do so. In the dressing room afterwards there was a real sense of accomplishment; a real sense of a well-earned victory, for a team that had suffered for years. As we gathered our thoughts, I asked the team captain to sing the song he had sung on the bus that day from Croagh Patrick.

We sat in a circle in the dressing room and he sang *"The Voyage"*; everyone to a man joined in on the chorus. It was a moment of beauty. We felt like Andy Dufresne's tarring crew in *"The Shawshank Redemption"*, drinking bottles of suds on the rooftop.

> *"We sat and drank with the sun on our shoulders, and felt like free men."*
>
> 'Red' (Morgan Freeman) in
> "The Shawshank Redemption"

That day, we sat in the dressing room and sang "The Voyage", and felt like free men. This new-found freedom, empowered us to have our most successful season in over a decade.

> *"With no maps to guide us we steered our own course*
> *Rode out the storms when the winds were gale force*
> *Sat out the doldrums in patience and hope*
> *Working together we learned how to cope*
>
> *Life is an ocean and love is a boat*
> *In troubled water that keeps us afloat*
> *When we started the voyage, there was*

just me and you
Now gathered round us, we have our own crew

Together we're in this relationship
We built it with care to last the whole trip
Our true destination's not marked
on any charts
We're navigating to the shores of the heart"

(The Voyage- Johnny Duhan)

Song is a powerful tool in the team environment…

.⌒ഴe⌒.

Last year, the Limerick Hurling Manager John Kiely once again climbed the steps of the Hogan Stand in Croke Park, Dublin to lift the Liam McCarthy Cup. This was his fifth time in six years to do so, but on this occasion a new energy appeared to come over him as he broke into exuberant celebration. It warmed the heart to see it, and the crowd went wild.

When asked later about his celebrations by Joanne Cantwell on The RTE Sunday Game, Kiely said:

"What ye don't realise is that the tune
that came on is one of our tunes in
the dressing room…. And when it goes off
in our dressing room, we go off with it,
so when it went off in Croke Park, I just

> *went off with it! So it didn't matter if there*
> *was nobody in the stadium, that was*
> *always going to happen!"*

The tune he was referring to was *"What do you want to know"* by Michael Maloney. Indeed, Maloney was invited to Limerick to perform that song for the team's homecoming celebration.

Song has the power to excite and unite…

·❧·

Many sports teams have adopted their own anthems: Munster Rugby have *"Stand Up and Fight"*, Liverpool FC have *"You'll Never Walk Alone"*, the Boston Red Sox have *"Sweet Caroline"*. Other teams adopt a song for a period of time. Leo Moran of *"The Saw Doctors"* tells of his surprise when he learned that the US Ladies Soccer team had adopted *"To Win Just Once"* (a song that was originally dedicated to the Galway Olympic boxer, Francis Barrett) for their World Cup campaign.

> *"To win just once would be enough*
> *For those who've lost in life and love*
> *… To win just once against the odds*
> *And once be smiled on by the gods*
> *To race with speed along the track*
> *Break the tape and not look back*
> *… To never have considered losing*

Song has the power to excite and unite.

As if to win is by your choosing
Bare your soul for all to find
An honest heart and an open mind"

('To Win Just Once'- Moran & Carton)

Song can be used to develop a real sense of mission.

.⁓ॐ⁓.

The Welsh Rugby Team are famous for their Team Choir. Throughout the various tenures of Head Coach Warren Gatland, the team have often engaged in singing, both as a way to build team spirit and a means to connect with their cultural heritage. Gatland, embraced and promoted this tradition as part of his team building strategy using song to enhance team morale and camaraderie.

.⁓ॐ⁓.

Along with song, simple song lyrics can also be used to move and influence the athlete. If a main player on a team I am involved with is coming back from injury or such, I will often send them the *Arcade Fires* song *"Intervention"* and ask them to listen to the first line,

"The King's taken back the thrown."

Another line I like to use with an athlete or team that are lacking true ambition is from *Pink Floyd's "Wish You Were Here."* In this song there is a line that says,

*"Did you exchange a walk-on part in the war,
for the lead role in a cage."*

Song is a powerful means to move people…

How can you use it to your advantage?

Go figure!

Being Part of the Solution

I designed *The CARVER Framework* as a set of lenses the coach could use to view their coaching practice through.

- Did I *Connect* to the player/ person?
- Did I *Connect* the players/ people to each other?
- Did I *Connect* the players/people to the game?

And so on…

Much of coaching is about perspective; it's about how you look at things. Through my writing, I strive to create pieces that can change the reader's perspective; help them look at things in a new light…from a new viewpoint. In coaching, our job is often to improve people's perspective; to change how they look at things.

Self-awareness in coaching is key. To paraphrase a Malayan saying:

> *'If you do not know what you do not know,*
> *then you won't know. If you do know what*
> *you do not know, then you will know.'*

Unfortunately, many coaches simply don't know, what they don't know, and this is a problem!

.୶ୡୡ୶.

Self-awareness in coaching is key.

Joe (aka VP) is one of the best coaches I know. He has a great blend of coaching skills…the full package. He is the real deal. He takes what he does seriously, but he doesn't take himself too seriously.

Joe finished his playing career, and went straight into coaching at a high level. He went in as second on a coaching ticket to Dave, who is a renowned coach; a special coach and a great mentor of mine. Dave is beautiful mix of fire and calm, patience and impatience, gentleness and directness, eloquence and bluntness. Often unknown to himself, Dave makes simple, yet profound, statements that can totally change your perspective.

Joe and I talk coaching at least two times a week. We chatted recently on the content of a piece I had written on the subject of *'ownership'*. Joe then told me of a one-liner Dave hit him with early in coaching career.

In advance of training one day, Joe was complaining to Dave about something or other to do with the performance of the players. That same day Dave wasn't in the mood for self-pity or soft-talk. He stopped Joe in his tracks, looked him in the eye and bluntly said:

"What are you gonna' do about it?"

Seven simple words in a questioning format…and then he walked away.

Joe is a perceptive fella with high levels of self-awareness. He quickly decked that his job was not to be critic or a fan. Being a *'problem identifier'* wasn't going to cut it if he wanted to cut the mustard with Dave. He would have to become a *'problem solver'*. He would have to become a real coach.

One question from Dave flipped his perspective and led him on a new coaching path where he'd take ownership of the fact that his role was to come up with solutions…not merely identify problems.

> *When we change the way we look at things,*
> *the things we look at change!*

What are you gonna' do about it?

Go figure!

Incorporating Traditional Wisdom into Coaching

Some years back I attended a Coaching Conference in Denver, Colorado. One of the speakers was Jerry Lynch, a veteran Sports Psychologist, Coach Educator and Author of several books on Coaching and Performance. Throughout his presentation Jerry referenced and leveraged a number of Buddhist and Native American teachings, and explained how they could be integrated into a coach's practice, and the team environment. I got talking to Jerry at the break, and enquired further into the content of his presentation. He commented that he thought I should look into Irish lore and culture. This resonated at some level.

Fast forward some years, and my American cousin Brian Kilgannon challenged me to use more Gaeilge (Irish) in my writing. Brian is a native of Brooklyn, New York. He was born to Irish parents in the 1950's, and has unique passion for life, learning and *'Éire'*. He has written an incredibly detailed Kilgannon family history, and has made an impressive effort to learn and use the Irish language. He is a man of amazing general knowledge, and has energy to burn. If you ever visit New York, I suggest you take a tour of *'The High Line'*, and Brian Kilgannon may well be your tour guide.

Anyway, here goes with Jerry and Brian's challenge to incorporate more Irish language and lore into my work...

An Irish Seanfhocal is a traditional proverb or saying that encapsulates the wisdom, humour, and values of Irish culture. They offer insights into life, human nature, and the world, conveying profound truths in a few words.

Below I have chosen ones I feel apply best to coaching. I trust that the prudent coach could well benefit from this wisdom.

- Fág an drochscéal san áit a bhfuair tú é.

Translation: Leave the bad story where you found it.
Coaching Wisdom: Keep positive, proactive and solutions focused. Don't confuse negativity with intelligence.

- Is maith an t-anlann an t-ocras.

Translation: Hunger is a great sauce.
Coaching Wisdom: Keep yourself, your athletes and your team hungry to learn, improve and compete. Challenge all parties to keep striving for their 'Best Self'.

- Más cam nó díreach an ród, 's é an bothar mór an t-aicearra

Translation: The longest road out is the shortest road home.
Coaching Wisdom: There are no short cuts.

Hunger is a great sauce.

- Molann an obair an fear

Translation: The work praises the man.
Coaching Wisdom: Stay humble. Focus on the work. Let it speak for itself.

- Tús maith leath na hoibre.

Translation: A good start is half the work/battle.
Coaching Wisdom: Set a strong foundation. In order to ensure long-term success, focus on the initial stages of training and development.

- Ní neart go cur le chéile

Translation: There is no strength without unity.
Coaching Wisdom: Create a culture of togetherness. Facilitate open and honest communication. Nurture alignment.

- An rud is annamh is iontach.

Translation: What is rare is wonderful.
Coaching Wisdom: Change things up on occasion.

- Giorraíonn beirt bóthar.

Translation: Two shorten the road.
Coaching Wisdom: Don't go it alone. Bring good people with you.

- Ní hé lá na gaoithe lá na scoilb.

Translation: The windy day is not the day for thatching.
Coaching Wisdom: Timing is everything. Don't force things.

- An té nach bhfuil láidir ní foláir dó a bheith glic.

Translation: He who is not strong must be clever.
Coaching Wisdom: Think strategically. Play to your strengths.

- Mol an óige agus tiocfaidh sí.

Translation: Praise the youth and they will flourish.
Coaching Wisdom: Encourage and support. Foster confidence and growth.

- Is fearr lúbadh ná briseadh

Translation: It's better to bend than to break
Coaching Wisdom: Be flexible when necessary.

And finally 3 light hearted, but never the less powerful, ones to finish…

- Ní dhéanfadh an saol capall rás d'asal.

Translation: You can't make a racehorse out of a donkey.
Coaching Wisdom: Challenge appropriately. Don't expect someone to do something they are incapable of doing.

- Is minic a bhris béal duine a shrón.

Translation: It is often that a person's mouth broke their nose.
Coaching Wisdom: Words have consequences. Choose them wisely.

- Nuair a bhíonn an t-ól istigh bíonn an chiall amuigh.

Translation: When the drink is in, the sense is out.
Coaching Wisdom: Leave the players and team to the heavy celebrations.

What traditional wisdom can you incorporate into your coaching?

Go figure!

The Power of Environment

One thing I know for sure about coaching is that:

Environment is the silent hand of behaviour.

In simple terms, people behave differently, in differing environments.

This learning was crystallised for me about 5 years ago, during my teaching days. Back then, our school was part of a pilot project which would see every child given a hot dinner for lunch. A pilot project, by its very nature, ensured it would involve a steep learning curve for the school community at large.

The process involved the children receiving their hot dinner 10 minutes before they were go out to yard for break. The teachers would go to their lunch in the staff-room, and the children were left to eat, with one teacher moving between a number of classes, to supervise and ensure general order was maintained.

One day, I was supervising the classrooms (4 in total) upstairs as they were eating. As I entered one of the 4th classes, I observed that very few children were eating the hot food provided; maybe 3 or 4 of the circa 25 children in the class. I then crossed the corridor to the other 4th class, and observed that the vast, vast majority of the children in this room were eating the hot food; maybe 23 of the circa 25 children. Curiosity got the better of me, and I began to question why

Environment is the silent hand of behaviour.

the same age-demographic of children, in the same school, being offered the same food, would behave so differently. In one classroom the behaviour was, *"We eat this hot food we are given for free."* While in the other classroom the behaviour was, *"We don't eat this hot food we are given for free."*

Searching for answers, I observed that the classroom where the children ate the hot dinner had a Special Needs Assist (SNA) in the room as the children ate. This lady was kind and motherly, and was liked and respected by the children. She also went over and above her job specification, which was to look after the needs of one child in the room.

In this classroom, the SNA in question would distribute the dinners, commend those who finished them, cheer those who had tried them or made an effort, challenge those who she felt could eat more and assist those who might need something cut up, or whatever. She would consistently recognise and acknowledge achievement and effort. Things that get recognised and acknowledged get repeated...I know that for sure. Her influence on the environment determined that the *emergent behaviour* was that...*"Around here, we eat our dinner."*

On the other hand, the classroom where the *emergent behaviour* was, *"We don't eat our dinner"*, had no such positive influence. The children ate or, more accurately, didn't eat, by themselves with little adult influence or support. I can only surmise that during the initial bedding in period of the project, one of the *'cool kids'* loudly announced that the dinner was *"crap"*. This would have gone unchallenged, and soon after a few *'impressionables'* most likely rowed in behind the theory. With that, the project was dead in the water in that classroom. As time went on, fewer and fewer ate the dinner, until it became almost impossible to eat it, such was the strength of the (negative) peer influence.

·⌒⌒·

I frequently enjoy sharing this story with coaches and it always resonates. As coaches we must constantly ask ourselves how can we engineer our practice and playing environment to ensure the desired behaviours emerge. And stick.

In other words, how can we make it so the children eat their dinner?

Go figure!

The Losing Game

I coached my first adult senior championship game at the age of 26 years old. It was with my home club, among my peers…and indeed my elders. We lost, and I wasn't prepared to lose.

Nowadays I coach coaches, and challenge them to be ready for the six possible scenarios they will face at the full-time whistle:

- *Played well and won.*
- *Played well and lost.*
- *Played poorly and won.*
- *Played poorly and lost.*
- *Played well and drew.*
- *Played poorly and drew.*

Players look to leaders for guidance, and the way forward, post-game. The prudent coach has a strong message prepared for all eventualities.

.⸜☙⸝.

Back then, I wasn't prepared, and found myself in the dressing room post-game, not knowing what to say. I ended up stumbling through a maxim I had heard, or read somewhere. It was:

$$E + R = O$$

Events + Response = Outcome

E+R=O
Events Plus Response Equals Outcome.

It is indeed a great maxim, but I delivered it poorly, and later that evening I heard it being bandied about in jest by players as they drowned their sorrows…embarrassing stuff indeed.

.⸲ᘐᓬ.

I attended a talk on *'Resilience'* a few weeks ago and the presenter used that same maxim. It brought me back to some of the toughest times in my coaching. Later that week, I had a session with a young coach I mentor. His team were on a long and hard losing streak. As our session unfolded, I was impressed by the strength of his *'response'* to the *'events'* of this losing streak. He forensically detailed how he is putting the microscope on his own coaching:

- *How he could improve the content of his sessions.*
- *How he could gain more insights from their video work.*
- *How he could put more focus on his one-to-ones…and so on.*

It was truly admirable to hear the fortitude he had in what was a challenging coaching position. He was searching for understanding; searching for answers.

He was focusing on what was under his control…he was being a real coach.

Losing is hard…but it is part of the gig. Marie Curie said,

> *"Nothing in life is to be feared, it is only to be understood. Now is the time to understand more, so that we may fear less."*

I think this logic applies to losing in sport.
The wise Stoic philosopher Seneca said:

> *"We suffer more often in imagination than in reality."*

Again I think this logic applies to losing in sport.

.⧈.

An acronym I like to use for losing is *LOSS.*

Learning Opportunity Stay Strong.

Just like *E+R=O, LOSS* is a useful way to frame your thoughts in times of challenge. **LOSS** can be a coaching perspective. Perspective is crucial in coaching

.⧈.

I met my young coach mentee again this week, and was delighted to hear that they had gotten a win at the weekend. The losing streak had tested both his coaching philosophy and coaching practice greatly, but he had stood strong to the challenge, and led by example through relatively tough times. Example is the only way to lead!

He had met the *'events'* of losing, with the *'response'* of self-reflection and self-improvement and the eventual *'outcome'* was that they got back to winning ways. He had *'stayed strong'* and used the loses as *'learning opportunities'*.

As a coach, how do you want to *'show up'* in times of loss?

Go figure!

Choosing Constraints Wisely

*(This essay was written in January 2024.
Owen Kilgannon passed away on May 25th
2024. His memory lives on!)*

I often reference John Wooden in my writing. Like many, I have been greatly influenced by his thinking and teachings. Wooden had some rules…

*"I had three rules for my players: No profanity.
Don't criticise a teammate. Never be late."*

John Wooden

I recently spent a week with my elderly cousin, Owen, in his house on Long Island, New York. Owen is 85 years old, with the spirit of a man half his age… and then some. I love spending time with Owen, his energy in the face of many physical ailments is a sight to behold. To paraphrase John Wooden, Owen never lets what he can't do, get in the way of what he can do.

.⌘.

Like Wooden, Owen has a rule in his house: No profanity. He argues that using profanity is a sign of a poor vocabulary.

Owen has a great turn of phrase. In coaching parlance, this, *'no profanity constraint'* he places upon himself (and others in his company) affords him the opportunity to find a variety of intelligent language solutions. In my line of work, words are important. To quote my famed mentor, Vern Gambetta, *"Words create images and images create actions."* As a student of words, I enjoy and appreciate Owen's phraseology.

Before I go any further I must disclose that I am a man who is prone to using profanity; I always have been. In my mind I don't use what I would term *'foul language'*, rather I use curse words as adjectives. Maybe it's an Irish thing; it's just something I've always done.

.⁓ৡৎ৶.

As I observed the constraint placed upon me while staying with Owen for that week, I began to reflect on the wisdom of Wooden's rule regarding profanity. I began to surmise that the rule acted as a constraint to afford his players the opportunity to find better ways to express themselves through language both inside, and outside of basketball. Now…whether this was Wooden's intention or not, I cannot say.

.⁓ৡৎ৶.

Language is important in coaching and performance. It is important for athletes as it enables them to articulate their views and opinions, as well as influencing their teammates. It is the foundation of social learning.

Shared language models and operational language helps drive the detail of performance.

One of my measures of coaching effectiveness is how well a player can describe what's happening in a game they are partaking in or observing. *Do they have the language of performance? Do they have the 'grammar' of the game? Is there detail to what they are saying? Can they articulate what they are observing?* Often the answer is no! Often you get basic words like: *good, bad or dare I say…"s&^t".*

A player or person-centred approach to coaching is key to improving the athlete's ability to articulate both themselves, and performance. Using questioning is a key methodology in this. As coaches we want *'students of the game'* and this challenges us to be professor like. Language is key to this. Finding interesting and engaging words and phrases to explain ourselves, our ideas and our game is critical.

.⟋⟍.

Owen's rule prompted me to reflect on Wooden's rule, and this got me thinking. Obviously, it's not as simple as having basic rules like *"no profanity"*; it must be underpinned by excellent coaching practices.

In conclusion, I suppose my thesis here is that the constraints coaches impose on their athletes may have farther-reaching effects than they appreciate.

The constraints coaches impose on their athlete may have farther-reaching effects than they appreciate.

There may well be unintended positive consequences at play.

How can you choose your language and constraints wisely?

Go figure!

Gaining Insights
through Conversations with
Fellow Coaches

The CARVER Framework positions coaching as a craft where perspective, tools and skills are the key drivers. My father was a carpenter, a craftsperson. He loved his craft; it was at the core of who he was as a person. The more I reflect on the craft of coaching, the more I see the parallels between the practice of coaching and how my father lived his life.

My father loved talking to fellow craftspeople: plumbers, plasterers, block layers, electricians, artists, potters and so on. He was at ease with them. They would talk about tools, materials, the quality of workmanship, and would go deep into conversation. One craftsperson would learn from another. They would share insights, which would in turn change their perspectives and way of doing things. It was lifelong informal education…social learning.

This week, I drove over 1,400 kilometres for my work in supporting coaches. I always aim to dovetail my travels with catching up with coaching buddies. This week, I caught up with many coaching buddies and had many coaching conversations.

First up I met Liam, a man affectionately known as "The Coaches' Coach". He gave me an insight into the old days in coach development, and how himself and

One craftsperson learns from another.

some buddies had worked together to raise the standard of coaching. Next I moved on to Noel; I actually stayed with him and his wife Orla and their kids. Their hospitality was first class. Noel works in Sports Medicine. He gave me a glimpse into his work with athletes, and the process that goes into early diagnosis and treatment of injury at an elite level.

The following day I had coffee with Peter who works in professional rugby and GAA. He is an athletic development coach with an engineer's mind. We talked broadly, yet deeply, about all things coaching and performance. I had lunch in Anne's house. She is a mindfulness coach. Present moment awareness is a key to performance across all domains. The present moment is where high performance is expressed. It was great to gain her insights into this area and the lunch was great too….all three courses. The following morning, I spent time with Philip. Philip specialises in player development. He's been at this game a long time. It is always uplifting to spend time with a great sage.

A few days later, I caught up with Paul. He is a hurling coach and also helps coaches improve. We talked about Lululemon trousers; among other things. I always admire his trousers; they look like a cross between a tracksuit bottom and chinos, and according to him they are extremely comfortable. They are the type of trouser you would get away with anywhere, on the pitch or afterwards in a social setting.

Later in the week I spoke with VP; I speak with VP a lot. He is a top class coach. His professional background is in change management and process improvement, and he is a fountain of insight and knowledge. Finally, I met Dave for tea, sometimes I call him 'Sensei'. Dave is an analyst, but he can coach a bit too. He is a numbers man. If I want to know what the facts of the matter are, I talk to him.

So, it was a week of travel and a week of very diverse coaching conversations; a week jam packed with informal learning. Sometimes as coaches we can look at the world through a straw; our perspective can be very limited and limiting. Coaching conversations change our perspective; the more diverse the better. Coaching conversation allow us to gain new insights and this allows us to change the way we look at things.

When we change the way we look at things,
the things we look at change.

To paraphrase that get Ghostbusters anthem…*"Who ya gonna call?"*

Go figure!

Taking Ownership

One of the great minds of humanity, the American theoretical physicist, Richard Feynman, famously said,

> *"The first principle is that you must not*
> *fool yourself- and you are the easiest*
> *person to fool."*

In coaching it is so easy to fool oneself. There is always the opportunity to blame someone else. Good coaches understand their role, and own the responsibility it brings; lesser coaches don't. The prudent coach must develop methods to save them, from fooling themselves.

Through my work I frequently meet coaches who, to paraphrase Feynman, are *'fooling'* themselves. This may sound harsh, and I really don't mean it to be so, but it is often the cold reality. Such coaches look for the solution to their problems externally, or in places that are outside of their control. In fact, often the reality is that their coaching practices are what are causing the problem, or similarly, improving their coaching practice is the solution to the problem. The tragedy is that such coaches are continually giving up the opportunity to change, grow and improve.

To quote George Washington Carver

"Ninety-nine percent of all failures come from people who have a habit of making excuses."

.⁓ঔ৹⁓.

This week I found myself reflecting on the titles of two books. The first book was written about the teaching principles and practices of the great John Wooden. This book, co-authored by Swen Nater and Ronald Gallimore, is called:

*"You Haven't Taught Until
They Have Learned"*

The second book is by two former navy seals, Jocko Willink and Leif Babin. The book is called:

"Extreme Ownership"

I really think these titles are great lenses for the prudent coach to look through. They say it all! In fact, one could mash them together, and add a few words of their own, in order to come up with the ultimate coaching perspective or truth.

*The prudent coach takes 'extreme ownership'
of the fact that they 'haven't taught
until the athlete has learned'.*

Leadership is about taking responsibility, not making excuses.

I acknowledge that this is easier said than done, but the alternative is to fool oneself. Leadership is about taking responsibility, not making excuses. Of course, in every sporting environment, there are things that the coach *'owns'* and things that they *'don't own'*. However, if we are to hold others accountable, we must first begin by holding ourselves accountable. After all…example isn't just another way to lead, it is the only way.

What do you *'own'* in your coaching environment?

Go figure!

Being of Service

My work involves quite a bit of travel. Travel involves interacting with people in the service industry; hotel staff, restaurant staff, retail staff and so on. I enjoy observing people in the service industry. I enjoy observing *how* they serve. I am currently writing this piece in a hotel restaurant. And, happily, the service is good.

We all like to be well looked after. We like to be met with a smile; made feel like our every need will be met. Poor service leaves a bitter taste, regardless of the *'cuisine'* on offer.

Coaching is a servant practice. As coaches we are there to serve the needs of the performer. Servant leadership is a leadership philosophy, where the leader's primary goal is to serve others. Rather than focusing solely on the accumulation of power or personal success, a servant leader prioritises the needs of their team members, empowering them to reach their full potential and achieve collective goals. Servant leaders understand that teams only thrive, when people thrive.

Through my work I preach servant practice. Expanding the footprint of my work in a congruent manner is something I have struggled with over the years, as I feel I cannot be self-serving in preaching servant practice. There is an ethical piece I need to thread carefully if I am to be truly authentic in my work. Obviously I need to *'sell'* in order to stay in business. Figuring out how to do this ethically and in a manner I am comfortable with, has been, and is, a challenge. An Irish seanfhocail which always springs to mind in this is:

> *"Molann an obair an fear."*
> *(The work praises the man.)*

I rarely get nervous when I present, but if I do, I like to use the following as a grounding mantra.

> *"If I am in service, I can't be nervous."*

I suppose what I am thinking in all this is that if I am coming from the *'right place'*, and have the required competencies for the task at hand, I cannot go wrong. To quote Nelson Mandela:

> *"A good head and good heart are always*
> *a formidable combination."*

Coming from the *'right place'* is key. We all must learn to come from *'our right place'* in coaching. I often explain to coaches that if I was giving them directions to a location, it would be worthless if I gave them the directions from my house. They must come from their own house, and to be of any value, the directions must orientate from *'their place'* not mine.

*In coaching we need to be more about,
"How can I help?"*

A recent observation I have made in the retail industry, is staff wearing t-shirts with slogans like:

Have a question?
Smiles & Service, On the Menu Everyday!
How can I help?
Here to Help!
Got Questions? I've Got Answers!
And so on…

In coaching we need to be more about, *"How can I help?"* We need to be more about service. If we come from *'this place'*, we really can't go too far wrong. Our focus should be on what we want *'for'* our athletes, as opposed to *'from'* them. Obviously, the more domain specific knowledge, skills and competencies we have the more impactful our work will be, but regardless of this, if we are coming from the *'wrong place'* we won't get to where we can. Our impact will not be as great as what it could.

I will end with a simple question for you to consider:

As a coach… what do you want
your 't-shirt' to say?

Go figure!

Noticing What You Want
to See

I am writing this essay on a runway of the Washington IAD airport on route to Park City Utah. My plane's take off has been delayed by 90 minutes. I am in America for two weeks working with a variety of organisations, coaches and athletes.

I have been pulling this piece together since my last visit to America over 5 months ago. Back then, I met a brain surgeon by the name of Anup. I had never met a brain surgeon before, and was keen to *'pick his brain'*. We spoke about many things, including: dealing with the pressure of surgery, and the workings of the brain's Reticular Activating System… but more of that later.

·⁓◦⁓·

Observation is a critical coaching skill. It provides the raw material for another key coaching skill: giving feedback. My personal preference is to be positive and precise in my feedback. *The CARVER Framework* encapsulates this practice through the *'Endorsing'* element. I like to notice and commend the *'good stuff'*: effort, improvement, learning, courage, effective skill execution, commitment and so on. I believe it is the best way to build confidence in those I work with. One thing I know for sure is that:

111

What gets recognised, gets repeated.

It is my belief that no coach intentionally sets out to be negative. For me, it is often the case that they don't possess the knowledge, skills, and self-awareness required to be positive. In general, positivity is good, but for me specificity in praise is key. Praise should not be vague, hollow or patronising. It should be as specific and rich in appropriate information. An example of this could be something like: *"Excellent head position in the tackle."* Precision in praise, leads to precision in performance, and precision is how you win.

Diligent research, introspection and self-awareness, will lead you, the coach, to appreciate and understand: human development and learning, skill acquisition and execution, the principles and concepts of your game and your *'Values and Visions'*. This, in turn, will lead you to understand what it is you want to notice in your athletes. Knowing what it is you want in, and from, your athletes, will empower you to commend or *endorse* it, as you notice it. After all, what we know determines what we see, and not the other way around. Knowledge and self-awareness, can enable you to be positive and precise in your praise. The *'good stuff'* is there if you are capable of noticing it.

·⌒∾⚬∾⌒·

Now, back to my brain surgeon buddy Anup and the *Reticular Activation System ('RAS')*. I like to explain

What gets recognised, gets repeated.

the skill of noticing through my understanding of the brain's *'RAS'*. Put simply, there is a network of nerves in your brain that control your state of awareness and attention. This system functions as a filter to accept and reject the overwhelming amount of stimuli that we all encounter when we are awake. You can actively set this *'filter'* by choosing to think about certain things, or it will be set by the environment.

In my coaching talks, I often share the story of designing the front wall of my house some years back. By that stage, I had been 32 years on this planet, and had pretty much never noticed a front wall. However, when it came that I had to design my own front wall, all I could notice were walls, and as the project commencement date drew closer, the more detailed my noticing became. I found myself noticing the height of walls, the stone in walls, the joints in the stonework of walls, the shape and position of the entrance of walls, and so on. At 32 years of age, I was only now noticing walls I had passed almost every day of my life. Why was that? It was because I had set my *'RAS'* to look for front walls.

Another, more recent personal example, is that of the commercial transportation choice of, friend of these essays, *'The Quare Hawk'* (see *'Making the Desired Behaviours More Attractive' page 19*). As a trades-man, 'equine entrepreneur' and father of 4, *'The Hawk'* was faced with commercial transportation conundrum when forced to replace his ailing Ford Transit Van. After a protracted negotiation with a private seller, he set-tled on a 2016, 5-seater, short-wheel base LDV V80.

This wagon is embellished with 5 spoke allow wheels, a large chrome bulbar, an oversized tow bar, and a rather fetching roof rack. It is quite the machine, and when loaded with his horse box is quite the sight as he cruises the *'mean streets'.* Long story short, since *'The Hawk'* purchased his new wagon, everywhere I go, I notice LDV vans. My guess is that they've always been there, but my *'RAS'* deemed them unimportant.

Through setting the *'RAS'* on what it is you want to see in your athletes, it is significant how powerful an impact it can have on your coaching practice. Better noticing will lead to better feedback and indeed better coaching in general.

A word of caution: it is that simple, but not that easy. You need to know your stuff, you need to be self-aware and you need to actively want to know the truth, and strive for improvement.

I will end with an insight from the Educational Researcher John Hattie:

*"To be effective, feedback needs to be clear,
purposeful, meaningful and compatible
with students' prior knowledge and
to provide logical connections."*

The devil is in the detail…What is it you want to notice in your athletes?

Go figure!

Planning for Success

I recently spent the afternoon in Byrant Park, Manhattan, with a buddy of mine who works as a New York City Planner. We were surrounded by all sorts of people, doing all sorts of things. Some were playing chess, others were reading in the outdoor *'Reading Room'*, some were playing a game called shuffle, while more were playing table tennis.

At the opposite side of the park, there were people sitting listening to a jazz band, while others were busy drawing and colouring at the *'Artists' Tables'*. That night, there was to be an outdoor cinema, on the beautifully manicured grass. Bryant Park is quite the place. It is evident that much planning and consideration has gone into making it so.

Along with people, we were surrounded by skyscrapers. The conversation with my New York City Planner buddy soon shifted to the planning process in Manhattan. In essence, I was enquiring about the process of a pretty regular tall building, being acquired by someone with a vision, and it subsequently being transformed into a skyscraper. I was full of questions: *What is involved in getting planning permission? What permits do you need to complete the work?* And so on…

In Manhattan, planning is big business. The process of building a skyscraper involves a feasibility study, site acquisition, design and planning, regulatory approvals and financing. It is only then, that the *'real work'* begins.

.⁓ঌ৹ৎ⁓.

Planning is also big business in coaching. To quote Dwight E. Eisenhower:

> *"Plans are nothing, but planning*
> *is everything."*

The prudent coach uses planning to deliver on their *'Visions'*. In order to be of any true value, all planning activities need to be aligned to a comprehensive and far reaching plan...a *'bigger picture'*. Effective planning cannot take place in a vacuum. Session plans must be connected to the previous session and, in turn, linked to the next session...ad nauseam.

I always say that in effective session planning, coaches should be able to justify every piece of their content. All content should have a direct link to the *'big picture'*. Variety can be nice, but in essence we need to create comprehensive programmes that have a high volume of what we deem to be the *'most important things'*. I am constantly challenging coaches to create sessions that are designed to deliver on their *'Visions'*.

Effective session planning is certainly not about copying or imitating others; your work should be a be a product of your own conclusions. Of course you can borrow ideas. We all do that!

In effective session planning, coaches should be able to justify every piece of their content.

As per *The CARVER Framework*, your session plans should embody:

- *Your Values*
- *Your Vision for your Athletes and Team*
- *Your Vision for your Coaching Team*
- *Your Vision for the 'Emotive State' in which you want your players to play in*
- *Your Vision for your Style of Play or Game Model*

Each session should have a *broad session objective* which should be directly related to your *'Values and Visions'. Age*-related considerations must be appreciated. Context is King! The *coaching techniques and methodologies* you intend to use also require thought.

Effective coaching sessions must always have the appropriate *physical, technical/ skill, tactical/ team play and mental challenge*s. Sessions should have organisation, enjoyment, learning, competitiveness and conditioning. Practice must prepare athletes for tough situations.

Content is critical, as is the application of your athletes.

How an athlete and team practices,
defines who they are.

Our role as coach is to ensure we optimise our session delivery so that that we empower the athlete to apply themselves to the best of their ability. This, too, must be planned for. Athletes are analytical creatures, who thrive on clarity.

For each piece of content, you should be able to clearly articulate and explain the following:

- *WALT* stands for *'We are learning to'*. You can use this concept to help raise your athletes' awareness of what they are doing and why they are doing it. Connect everything to the game, the principles and concepts of the game, and performance improvement. Show them where it fits in. They need to know... *Why.*

- *WILF* stands for *'What I'm looking for'*. You must know and effectively articulate exactly what you're looking for in each activity. Example, can also play an important role here.

- *Key Coaching Points (KCPs)* and *Coaching Cues*- What are the *KCP's* of the skills and the cues for coaching them?

*"I never tell a player this is my way now
do it. Instead, I say, this is the way we do it,
and this is why we do it."*

Vince Lombardi

Appropriate *questions* should also be prepared. *Timings* are also important: How long are you going to spend at each section? How long are you going to allow for transitions from one exercise to the next?

.ᴈᴈᴈ.

Skyscrapers don't just appear in the sky after a physical effort. Behind this physical effort is a rigorous planning and preparation process. Similarly, great athletes and teams don't just appear on the podium.

*'Plans are nothing, but planning
is everything.'*

How can you plan for success? Your *'Vision'* of it, of course!

Go figure!

Using Words to Create Images and Actions

(This essay was written in April 2024)

*"Words create images, and images
create actions."*

This is a lesson I learned from one of my mentors, the famed Vern Gambetta.

As coaches, not only must we be mindful of what we say, but we must also be mindful of how we say it. Our ability to articulate both ourselves, and our thoughts and ideas, can be a coaching superpower. The game is about the images that are in our players' heads. Our words can be a means of painting the most vivid of images.

The great coach, John Wooden was famed for his articulate use of words; so much so that the phrase *'Woodenisms'* has entered popular coaching vernacular. A *'Woodenism'* refers to the insightful sayings and aphorisms he repeatedly used to drive home his message. For example:

*"Do not let what you cannot do, interfere
with what you can do."*

"Be quick, but don't hurry."

Words create images, and images create actions.

*"Things turn out best, for those who make
the best of the way things turn out."*

'Woodenisms' are celebrated for their simplicity and depth. In a few brief words, they offer guidance on how to be successful in both sport, and life.

.⌒᷾ᴥ᷾⌒.

I believe how we use words in coaching is integral, so much so, that I made it one of the core elements of *The CARVER Framework* i.e. *'Endorsing'.* Some time back, in the early days with a team I was coaching, we experienced a very chastening day, where we were simply bullied off the field by a rival team. Yes, the opposition crossed the line regarding the rules and spirit of the game but, none the less, it was crucial that we diagnosed exactly what had happened: We had been preyed upon. After that day we came up with some words…a saying,

"We are the hunters… Never the hunted."

These words were used to create the image of the *"hunter mentality"* and this served us well throughout the lifetime of that team. Yes, there were days we came out the wrong side of the result, but thereafter I can honestly attest that there was never a day when we were *"the hunted"*.

> *"Words create images, and images
> create actions."*

In his second coming as Donegal Gaelic Football manager, Jim McGuinness crash-landed back into the collective consciousness of the GAA community last weekend, with his team's resounding defeat of the much fancied Derry. McGuinness is an enthralling character who appears to understand the value of words and imagery. Indeed, the title of his 2015 autobiography *"Until Victory Always"* was a direct nod to the legendary rebel Che Guevara's famed saying *'Hasta La Victoria Siempre'*. In choosing these words, McGuinness was conveying the ideas of rebellion, defiance, irreverence, the underdog and indeed, glorious victory.

Of what we see from the outside, McGuinness uses words really well. Some weeks back in an interview with Highland Radio he used the phrase, *"decisions and incisions"* when referring to the moments when his players were in possession. The word *"incisions"* was new to me in this context, but it paints such a vivid picture of surgically cutting through the opposition's defence. *Penetration* or *breeching* have been words that have been widely used in this context, but here he was utilising an even more refined word, and using rhyme to dovetail it with another key area of the game, namely decision making. On the ball, their game would be all about, *"decisions and incisions."*

Last week after the defeat of Derry, McGuinness said he was delighted that his team was able to bring *"the level that is required."* The use of this phrase is interesting, as it is objective and matter of fact; it doesn't depend on any external factors, or influences.

He then went onto talk about the *"transitional moments"* being so valuable and hard got. The common coaching vernacular here is usually *'the transition'*, but he was using the phrase *"transitional moments"* to make them ever more vivid, more valuable and more special.

He finished by saying he was delighted that the *"passion and drive"* was there among his players to get up the field to *"support each other"* in these *"transitional moments".* In using these words, he was glorifying and extolling the raw human endeavour required to be a true team.

> *"Words create images, and images
> create actions."*

How do you wish to use yours?

Go figure!

Nurturing Virtues for Sport and Life

I have written about the life, and work, of the late George Washington Carver in *'Determining and Detailing Your Visions'* on page 7. Carver was a revolutionary African American agricultural scientist, inventor and academic who spent 47 years teaching at what is now Tuskegee University.

Like all good teachers and coaches, Carver was as much concerned with his students' personal development, as he was with their intellectual development. To clarify his thinking, he compiled a list of *"eight cardinal virtues"* whose possession defines *"a lady or a gentleman"*. He surmised that these virtues were required for the student to rise to the *"full height of their possibilities"*. These virtues were as follows:

1st. *Be clean, both inside and out.*

2nd. *Who neither looks up to the rich, nor down on the poor.*

3rd. *Who loses, if needs be, without squealing.*

4th. *Who wins, without bragging.*

5th. *Who is always considerate of women, children and old people.*

6th. *Who is too brave to lie.*

7*th*. *Who is too generous to cheat.*

8*th*. *Who takes his share of the world, and lets other people have theirs.*

The CARVER Framework counsels that our work as coaches should be crafted and designed to help deliver on our *'Visions'.* One *'Vision'* I always challenge coaches, clubs and organisations to detail and define is their *'Vison for the Athlete'.* There are two parts to this *'Vision',* namely: *The Sporting and Non-Sporting Qualities of the Athlete.* Similarly, this could also be described as, a *Vision for the Athlete and the Person*, or a *Vison for the Performance and Personality Qualities.*

Each sport, and indeed playing position within each sport, will require differing physical, technical, tactical and mental qualities of the athlete. These are the sports-specific qualities. However, the desired personal or non-sporting qualities are universal across all sports, and indeed performance domains. These are the qualities G. W. Carver referred to as *'Virtues'.*

I have spent quite some time ruminating on, and detailing, the *'Virtues'* I feel the athlete will require to make the best of their athletic abilities, or to quote G.W. Carver, reach the *"full height of their possibilities".* In my opinion it is only when the coach, club or organisation is clear on the *'Virtues'* they wish to nurture in their athletes, that they can go about designing and developing a comprehensive, and effective, body of work that can be delivered over the expanse of time. If, *'Rome wasn't built in a day'*, I can guarantee you, neither was an athlete who is capable of maximising their athletic potential.

Below I detail, in the linguistic style of the great G. W. Carver, what I will reverently term *'The Eight CARVER Cardinal Virtues'*.

1st. *Who is of High Character*

To quote Bill Belichick, *"Talent sets the floor, Character sets the ceiling."*

2nd. *Who is Self-Managing*

The athlete must learn to own their own *'stuff'*. Organisational skills are invaluable. The self-managing athlete is the empowered athlete.

3rd. *Who is a Pro-Active Learner*

One's only sustainable competitive advantage is to learn faster than the opposition. Learning skills are critical. If we are open to learning, we are on the right track.

4th. *Who is a Clear & Critical Thinker*

Good thinking, leads to good doing.

5th. *Who Lives a Balanced & Healthy Lifestyle*

Sleep, diet, rest and downtime are necessary for intense application and growth.

6th. *Who is Intrinsically Motivated*

No one can learn for the athlete, and no one can practice or perform for them. They have to want it for themselves.

7th. *Who is Intentioned*

Much of reaching one's potential involves remaining focused and avoiding distraction. Goal setting is a great way to focus the athlete. Intentionality is key.

8th. *Who is Consistent*

Consistency beats intensity. Enduring performance is built day by day, week by week, month by month and year by year.

With your *'Vision'* clear, reasoned and well-articulate the coaching challenge becomes to design a programme of work and a playing environment that can build, and nurture, the skills, competencies and qualities required to realise this *'Vision'*.

An example of such work in practice is that of the great All Black team who won back-to-back Rugby World Cups in 2011 and 2015. Their guiding principle that *"Better People Make Better All Blacks"* was detailed by James Kerr in the famed book "*Legacy*". This principle, that character and integrity off the field, enhances performance on the field, was established in the 2000s when the All Blacks, under the stewardship of leaders such as Graham Henry, focused on developing humility, accountability, and continuous self-improvement within their ranks.

One of the team's, by now, well-renowned rituals that encapsulated this philosophy, was that of *'sweeping the sheds'*. Although, this practice has been mimicked the world over, out of context, and with little or none of

*The true power of sport is that it should act as a
vehicle to 'get better' at life.*

the required foundational work in place, does not take away from the authentic symbolism it represented for the mighty All Blacks. As detailed by Kerr in *"Legacy"*,

> *"While the country is still watching replays*
> *and school kids lie in bed dreaming*
> *of All Black glory, the All Blacks are*
> *tidying up after themselves…Sweeping the*
> *sheds…Doing it properly…So no one else*
> *has to…Because no one looks after the All*
> *Blacks…The All Blacks look*
> *after themselves.*

There you have it: self-managing athletes!

.⸎⸎⸎.

Earlier in this piece I noted that the non-sporting qualities are somewhat universal across all sports and indeed performance domains. In this, I mean that these qualities will transfer into all areas of the athlete's life. I have often said that the true power of sport is that it should act as a vehicle to *'get better'* at life. This places a huge societal sway on you coach…See what you can do for them…

What do you see as the *'Virtues'* you wish to nurture in your athletes? What is your *'Vision'*?

Go Figure!

The Value of Sport

The Mission of *CARVER Coaching and Performance* is to improve the standard of coach, performer, and team support for performance and societal benefit. The societal piece is important to me. To quote the great South African Leader, Nelson Mandela:

"Sport has the power to change the world."

My work affords me the opportunity to meet a significant volume of coaches. Some are professionals, while others are volunteers. Currently, I meet and work with in excess of 100 volunteer coaches weekly. These are predominantly good people trying their best, often poorly equipped and supported in challenging environments. It continues to resonate with me the influence these people hold...the power they have to improve our society.

Two weeks ago, I was asked in an interview if I was the national head of sports coaching, what would I do. My answer was that I would aim to elevate the status of the *'ordinary coach'*. I would start a *'coaching awareness campaign'*. How I would do this is for another day, and is no doubt easier said than done.

In the past, I have been asked to sit on round-table discussions in hospital and healthcare settings. I have been there to be a voice for sport and coaching. Doctors, psychologists, nutritionists, and other

Sport has the power to change the world.

healthcare professionals have sat with me. In my humble opinion, my message has been simpler and more powerful than the rest. My message has been that if we improve the standard of volunteer sports coaching, we will improve many and most of society's ills; obesity, mental health issues, addiction, and so on. For me, it is simple and clear: The *'ordinary coach'* holds the key to unlocking the extraordinary potential of sport. Of course, there is no such thing as an 'ordinary' anything.

Sport, at its most morally praiseworthy, is a place of human endeavour. It is a place where learning and development come about through challenge. Sport is a place to explore the limits of human potential and to maximise what we have been given. At its most moving and noble, sport doesn't have to involve cups, medals, or money. It can and should provide the opportunity to both exhibit and develop great moral courage, to find enjoyment, connection, and meaning. Those with influence in sport hold significant societal sway. Traditional wisdom tells us that being involved in sport is good for our youth, but are we maximising its potential?

Sport must offer a place for everyone: from the elite to the recreational, from the gifted to the not so gifted. Sport is not just for the talented, the champions, and the early developers. Sport must be for everyone, and from this environment, the individual will emerge to find their level if coached appropriately.

Sport provides endless opportunity, and opportunity is the mother of all learning and development. For me, the primary role of sport is to teach young people lessons for life:

'Try your best, learn as you go, improvement comes through challenge and application, stick together, learn how to win and lose with dignity'.

Sport should be a vehicle to help people develop themselves and strengthen their constitution for this world. When the learner is guided appropriately, sport gives them the opportunity to develop mental and physical resilience, character, communication and teamwork skills, as well as leadership qualities. This all sounds idyllic, however, the reality can often be the opposite when the leadership isn't competent. Sport can often be about the negatives of elitism, aggressive and disrespectful behaviour, abusive supporters, and so on.

As coaches and leaders, it is our great challenge to lead with nobility and help optimise the value of sport. This is a big order! Sport needs us! Society needs us! Coaches are the ones who can curate the conditions which allow the *'good stuff'* to happen. The *'great stuff'*.

We must strive to provide an environment that protects the weak, challenges the strong, and ensures our athletes are treated with respect, afforded opportunity, and challenged appropriately. We must create a climate where the athlete is allowed to express themselves, extend themselves, and evolve their own style and personality. In *"Be the Best You Can Be in Sport- A Book for Irish Youth"*, my good friend 'The Coaches' Coach' Dr. Liam Moggan summed it up beautifully when he said:

> *"If future generations are to be liberated*
> *and to thank us, we need to feed their*
> *passion and enthusiasm and integrate*
> *fun and enjoyment into the wonderful world*
> *of sport. We need to encourage people*
> *to do something they enjoy rather than*
> *be better at doing something*
> *than someone else".*

What do you see as the value of sport and how do you intend to play your role in maximising it?

Go figure!

The Power of One's 'Why'

Approximately 5 months ago I sat with a coaching buddy of mine called Padraic. We were shooting the breeze about coaching and life, and he mentioned my newsletter. He said that in particular, he enjoyed the *'CARVER Insights'* piece.

Up until my chat with Padraic, the newsletter had two parts. The first part was a relatively rudimental, informative piece on a coaching or performance topic, while the second part was what I termed a *'CARVER Insight'*. In essence, a *'CARVER Insight'* was my own personal take on some coaching topic or other, and it was delivered in what I felt was an engaging, narrative style. Occasionally, the *'Insight'* would simply consist of an update on where I had been, and what I was working at.

Long story short, as I began to develop the *'CARVER Insight'* concept I really enjoyed writing the pieces, and in *'Season 1'* I wrote about 15 *'Insights'* that I felt were of high quality. As *'Season 2'* began, I continued with the same structure: *Information piece* to start followed by a *'CARVER Insight'*. Again, some *'Insights'* were on the money, while others were of minimal value to the reader. It was a time and energy thing, a quality *'Insight'*, was tough to land.

All of this changed after my chat with Padraic. You see, Padraic said something that day changed the purpose of my writing. Up in until then I had been producing work, but my purpose, or vision, for it wasn't as clear as it needed to be. Sure, I wanted to help coaches and took pride in producing work of a certain standard, but it was proving a great challenge. I was spending hours on it every week, and the newsletter was free to readers. I am self-employed and there are many, many challenges to being a self-employed performance coach in sport and the workplace. It is an infant industry, and many are only beginning to appreciate its value.

.ഹോ.

So what did Padraic say that changed everything? Padraic loosely said that he thought I should make a book of my *'CARVER Insights'*.

As soon as he said it…I was all over it. From then on I would produce *'CARVER Insights'* of the highest standard I possibly could, and incorporate them into a book. This book would have the potential to go all over the world, make a genuine impact, and be available to people for years and decades to come.

.ഹോ.

Since I have set my heart on a *'CARVER Insights'* book, the quality and consistency of my writing has improved. My purpose has driven my performance. I have delivered every week throughout a pretty hectic period of work, travel and family life. There were many weeks when I thought of giving it a skip and making an excuse, but I stuck at it. There were many Friday's when I hadn't the piece to the standard that I was happy with, but I crawled onwards, and got it over the line.

My writing process has improved…I have established the habits and behaviours required to deliver week on week. In general, I will have 8 or 10 ideas out ahead of me at all times and will be slowly growing *Word* documents on these ideas. If I see something associated with a topic, I throw it into the *Word* document, and when I feel I have enough insight and raw material gathered I go about writing it; word by word, line by line.

These pieces don't simply just flow out of me. There is a long, painstaking process involved, and in order for me to endure this process, my purpose must be very strong. To paraphrase Viktor E. Frankl in *"Man's Search for Meaning"*,

"When your 'why' is strong enough, you can bear with almost any 'how'."

I feel I am being honest with people when I say that coaching is tough. This is why I always challenge them to reflect deeply on their *'why'*.

When your 'why' is strong enough, you can bear with almost any 'how'.

What is the *'why'* in your coaching, and is it strong enough to bear the 'how'?

Go figure!

P.S. The book I am referring to in this piece is the very book that is in your hands.

The end is always the beginning

Thanks

Thanks to Noel Napier, Liam Moggan, Giles Warrington, Liam Brady, Dinny Stapleton, Niall McElwee, Gary Sice, Declan Varley and Shane Curley for their feedback on these essays, and input into the project.

Thanks for Lucia Balazova for her great illustrations.

Thanks to Lauren and Rían for their love and support. Our journey continues.

Thanks to my family and friends for putting up with me.

Thanks to all those who have read and supported the CARVER Coaching and Performance Newsletter. This book wouldn't have happened without you.

Thanks to anyone who has supported my work in any way. I really do appreciate it.

Viva La Revolution,
Paul

Other Books and Journals
by Paul Kilgannon

- Coaching Children in Sport- The CARVER Framework
- Be the Best You Can Be in Sport- A Book for Irish Youth
- Be the Best You Can Be in Sport- A Book for the Young Sportsperson
- Journaling to Be the Best You Can Be in Sport- A Journey into Journaling
- Be the Best You Can Be in Sport- The Daily Journal
- Be the Best You Can Be in Sport- The Weekly Planning and Reflection Journal
- Be the Best You Can Be in Training and Competition- The Performance Preview and Review Journal
- Be the Best You Can Be in Coaching- A Journal to Define, Refine and Deliver Your 'Coaching World'

Coming Soon

- Coaching in the Workplace- The CARVER Framework
- Insights for the Sports Coach Vol. 2 (hopefully 3 and maybe 4)

Find out more at

www.carercoaching.com

twitter and Insta: @carver_coaching

Facebook: Carver Coaching

Notes